FLICKER AND HAWK

FLICKER AND HAWK

PATRICK FRIESEN

TURNSTONE PRESS

Published with the assistance of the Manitoba Arts Council and the Canada Council.

Turnstone Press
607-99 King Street
Winnipeg, Manitoba
Canada R3B 1H7

This book was typeset by b/w type service ltd. and printed by Hignell Printing Ltd. for Turnstone Press.

Printed in Canada.

Cover art: "Couple" by Marsha Whiddon, oil on panel, 102 cm. x 150.5 cm.

Cover design: Steven Rosenberg

Back cover photo: Carol Friesen

Some of these poems have appeared in *Canadian Literature*, *event*, *Northern Light*, *Border Crossings*, and *CV/2*.

Canadian Cataloguing in Publication Data

Friesen, Patrick, 1946-
   Flicker and hawk

    Poems.
    ISBN 0-88801-113-X

    I. Title.

PS8561.R56F4 1987   C811'. 54   C87-098019-X
PR9199.3.F74F4 1987

contents

water burial

sunday afternoon

on sunday afternoons all the fathers in town slept
I think they dreamed of old days and death
sometimes you could hear them cry
the summer air was still at the window
flies on the screen and the radio playing softly in the kitchen

mother slid a fresh matrimonial cake onto potholders on the stove
picked up a book a true book of someone else's life
sunglasses a pitcher of lemonade and a straw hat
spread a blue blanket in the backyard near the lilac shrubs for
    shade
lay down one ear hearing children in the garden
she never escaped all the way nor did she want to not quite
this much on a sunday afternoon went a long way

downtown boys rode main street toward fiery crashes they imagined
twisted wrecks with radios playing
rock 'n' roll insulting the highway
townspeople gathered on the shoulder
standing as near as they could to the impossible moment between
    what's here and not

a girl's body sprawled in the ditch no one knew at first whose
    daughter she was
though someone pulled her skirt down for decency
the smell of alcohol and fuel everywhere
her lipstick so so red beneath the headlights
they couldn't take their eyes from her lips
what was she doing in a wild car like that? who was she?

at night I shivered in bed wondering how to get out of town
side-stepping wrecks they were everywhere on all the roads heading
    out toward the lights and laughter
a dented hubcap an amazing shoe with its laces still done up
    made you wonder how someone could step right out of a shoe
    like that like the flesh was willing or surprised or not there to
    begin with

in nightmares angry lords walked through my room
it took my breath away how ferocious love could be
sometimes jesus hung on the wall or was it the shadow of an elm?

in the morning at the kitchen table green tomatoes on the window
    sill we held devotions with careful hands
father's eyes focussed hard on me so he wouldn't remember but of
    course he did
listening often to mother's sunny childhood dreams
I thought I was free I was a child with a dancing mother
and my town was filled with children and my town had backstreets
    and sheds and black dogs and sugar trees but she disappeared
    and he died and I got out I'm getting out I'm getting out
what I left there the child gathering raspberries in an enamel bowl
he's not dead he went back to where you are before you're born
    again
waiting for the next time and another town

john isaacs is long gone

rilla epp's taken away her heat and john isaacs is long gone
damascus thessalonica such names
gethsemane curled around my tongue in flames
my world was a street and now I am the town

john isaacs drank a bottle every day and dreamed of france
someone said he'd been in the war
now he had nothing to live for
when the salvation army band played he marched and danced

evenings you could see mrs gerbrandt at prayer through the glass
I heard she had nerve trouble
she couldn't stop seeing double
she wasn't sure of salvation and her days were as the grass

j j schellenberg was in church when his wife tumbled down the
        stairs
six sons carried her away
four daughters knelt to pray
schellenberg sat in his study and wept as he remembered her hair

there was a yellow house and rilla epp whose dress was tight
all afternoon she raked leaves
she piled them to the eaves
when her husband was away she made bonfires all night

my world was a street and now I'm the town
damascus thessalonica such names
gethsemane curled around my tongue in flames
rilla epp's taken away her heat and john isaacs is long gone

birthday dream diary

monday went to work at 7
it rained all day
got home at 7
rain stopped so we went for walk

tuesday
brought ice cream home at noon
for my sweetie

wednesday very hot
mary and henry for supper
hoed in garden after

father's gardens were diligently shaped
not obsessively nor with insolence
but with honour
and the fear honour authenticates

the garden was his sculpture
how he baffled the unacknowledged
and adored what his hands knew

thursday warm out
margaret washed floor and polished
had supper
margaret tired tonight

friday margaret woke with pains
walked to hospital about 2 a m
baby was born about 4
I went to see margaret
happy to see her in her smiling face

he couldn't know it was a last dream
he was young and strong
though he understood the natural world
he had forgotten how it would claim him

there was always the garden's arrangement and eternity's prospect

saturday went to work at 7
went to mom and dad for supper
I went to margaret after 7
brought her bars and flowers
left her with a kiss and bye-bye

it was a last dream
as if sunday might never arrive
with its change of clothes
its sermon
and its afternoon sleep

it fooled him his hands
how quickly things went
he was working the whole day long
that's what a man did with his strength
digging measuring the earth for home

it fooled him how quick it was
another world war over
his lucky marriage his firstborn
nativity a moment of his flesh leaping past
the boy with big eyes and long legs and words
the boy a man suddenly beside his father's bed
neither understanding the other's failure

always he had his dignity
it was something no one could take from him
with a shaky hand he combed his thin hair for death
it was close to a dream
father's alabaster skull
and one last possible day for remembering

sunday it's a very nice day
john toews brought the sermon
drove home after
passed the hospital
saw my sweetheart waving from her window
had raspberries for dinner
went to hospital to see my lover
but not just to see her
but to bring her a kiss

wedding music

mother took off her wedding ring
and laid it on the piano

she leaned sideways
to see if her foot was on the right pedal

she clenched and unclenched
her hands above the keyboard

then   as she swayed toward the music sheet
her fingers descended like snow

I saw the white skin on her finger
where her marriage had been

bible

the bible was a telephone book
of levites canaanites and reubenites
it was a television set
my favourite program being revelation
until someone told me what it meant

the bible whispered to itself at night
I thought I heard the song of solomon and lamentations
maybe job   and later second thessalonians
in the morning there were always new underlinings

it was a vacuum cleaner once
a week later it was a close shave

the bible was a cockroach
scuttling its dark way through the house
would it survive the holocaust?

it was a black dog behind the couch
I could see its muzzle from where I sat at the piano

the bible took me aside
and taught me how to squint
it grasped my hand
and showed me how to shake

once
I remember it was fall
the bible took me to a show
of time-lapse photography

you could see flowers open in seconds
wounds and mouths and skies
a city strayed from dawn to night in a moment
you could almost hear it cry
or maybe it was someone in the crowd

the bible was a whorehouse
leaning at the edge of the world
I took some pleasure there
had regrets

I could say the bible taught me everything
but I remember how I once threw my life away
when I was unafraid and prodigal
I wish it would happen again

and though I don't quite believe it myself
this afternoon   while I was going through my photographs
I heard the bible laugh

song of the sly one

I am the man
who will solve your problems
without a thought
and if you have fish
I will show you
where they were caught

I am a monk
who slipped his vows
and never prayed
look behind you
look ahead
I'm standing in your shade

I am the liar
every father dreads
and every mother claims
where you have a court
where you have opinion
I will take the blame

I am a sly one
who slides through the net
that every jesus cast
show me an icon
show me the text
I will show you where I passed

fool's week

a day like any other

monday morning I felt
like not going to work
for no reason
so I didn't

slept all morning
dishes in the afternoon

on tuesday
I put God out
with the cat

house was empty for a bit
soon filled it with silence
not to say a drink or two

it was wednesday
at a committee meeting
I made a fool of myself
and everyone else
I hope

slept well

I disregarded doctor's advice
all day thursday
felt fine
in a way

had people over at night
I impersonated and ridiculed
a famous conductor
who recently slept in my basement
because of the drought

forgot an important birthday friday
didn't sleep well
all the memories I hadn't asked for
not to mention the alcohol
which had no place to go
and settled in with me for the night

on saturday
I thought of doctors
a moment of weakness

wrote a sad poem for my town
it seemed all that was left

went to sleep
with a full moon splashing
on my eyes

I dreamed of flying wallendas

sunday morning I woke
to what I thought could be my last day
or the first
everything clear
wondered if I would ever learn
to forget everything I knew

realized I didn't have to

I was becoming light
on a sunday
with all the other days before me

ghost

grandfather didn't want anyone to know he was going
he held the news sweetly and told his stories
who would have guessed he could leave just like that
giving up the way a man of humour will
the way a person faces what was dreamed long ago
who would have guessed it on a dreary afternoon
snow falling and curtains trifling with light

he used to look aside cocking his ear
like a blind man listening the words just slipped away
I knew him I'd stake my life on it
even in death I knew him he was growing young
all his 76 years count them he blew them out

in his basement he reached for a bottle in the beams
he raised a glass and asked had I met the ghost
he knew it well talked with it often while grandmother slept
sometimes in the basement sometimes in the kitchen
he'd be sitting with a paperback and smokes
next thing he knew there it was the ghost
said it told him everything he needed to know and then some

he chuckled that cigarette chuckle
said pretty well everything was an outright lie or the truth
stirring his coffee   *you know?*   he looked up
the spoon going around   *you know?*

and him smiling in the easy chair beneath the lamp

first light

there are fingers growing in the garden
between potato plants and along the hedge

the wind sighs at the back door
a shadow passes among the raspberry canes

someone's on the roof
shouting   a prodigious voice
on his knees in the garden a man looks up
smiling in surrender

the shed door bangs shut
a woman's kerchief sails away

the sun's going down
walls are white
and the windows black

inside the children are dreaming toward first light

beneath the willow

children chew leaves and blossoms
they eat trees whole   and gardens

there is a lie I need to know
I lean hidden in the doorway

his hands dreaming in their pockets
my son lingers in the shade

beneath the willow
there's no place to go

I close the door softly not to wake him
my mouth is bitter from lilac stems

the lawn lies clipped and nervous
above tonight's fulmination

warrior

1.

crouching in long grass
in france in november
descartes in his pocket

he was watching the railroad
the train was late
and everything silent
meaning he heard war far away

2.

he walked around the town
it was deserted
he heard the echo of a bell

like moonlight on water
like smoke at the window

3.

nothing compared to anything
nor stood for something else

he was thinking of home
white stones bordering a flower garden

he was thinking of his sister
the song they used to sing on christmas eve
he could almost hear the words

he reached into his pocket for the photographs

4.

I am here
on bastille boulevard
he thought
nowhere else

how could the photographs be true?

he laid them down
one by one
on paving stones

when he glanced back
still able to see them
he thought they were his footprints
but they weren't

he knew that in a way
it was just a thought

5.

a wound on his foot was festering
it reminded him of the time he stepped on a nail
in july when he was nine

the day before
on his birthday
he had posed with his new bicycle

grandmother had soaked a rag in sour cream
and wound it around his foot

he was looking for a dispensary
or a barbershop with a surgeon's pole

6.

the room was filled with broken mirrors
a hat hung on a hook
and a razor lay in the shattered glass

he sat in the chair
thinking of all the men
who had been there before

their hair was on his sleeves

he remembered every man he had killed
and the woman whose shadow he saw in a window

it troubled him
how he saw motion
he fired and knew
it was a woman's shadow he had seen
her long hair
her cry
but when he broke down the door no one was there

he thought the floor was spattered with blood
but it was light through stained glass

the room was bare except for a mirror leaning against a wall
he felt she was near   he spun around the room
there was no hole the bullet should have made
the mirror was frightening   who knew what it had seen

night was falling   there was moonlight in the street
he stood and brushed the hair from his sleeves

7.

it was the smell of rain in fall
he would take to his grave
the way   when he was a boy   rain sometimes fell all day
how he thought it would blow the house away

though he dreamed all night of paradise
in the morning the house was always there
and sometimes the rain was too

he shivered
as if he had eaten a gooseberry
he thought

he broke his reflection in a rain barrel
to wash his face

he sat down on a bench
drew his greatcoat about him
this was his place for the night
he was humming *stille nacht*
and smiling in the rain

poem for smiling broken hearts
for jane casey

your clothes fall to the floor
you stand beside the window
will such pale lips ever speak?

often you incline your head   bemused
or listening from a distance
a mother watching the child at her breast

you are the only one with your smile
look around   there are faces that love you
but none has your smile
its demure grace   it affirms your silence
a memory of mother's footsteps

it was when she loved you all afternoon
in october   rain and leaves on the lawn
she sat beside you sleeping on the rug

she touched you   it wasn't a dream
or it was the dream waking for a moment
a divided water   the curtain torn

her fingers blessed your eyelids
and tucked brown hair behind your ears

the dream returning
was her footsteps walking into another room
this happens   houses empty   leaving walls and doors

these days there is a handkerchief in your hands
there are angels in your eyes

janey jane   there are feet inside you
they're cutting across lawns
you're listening   aren't you?

there are feet all around

water burial
for les brandt

whether it's a july afternoon
and you're swimming off patricia beach
knowing this is the inheritance you were born to
or you're listening to the blue ridge rangers
singing you toward the home you imagine
or you're stealing an afternoon from necessity
you are on your way to salvation
if not already there

on the other hand
how easily the body drifts away sometimes
dreams or disease mishap or sloth

or something else
voices at night
I remember that
a nearly full moon drooping into the lake
and shadows on the pier
children and women talking in the embrace of the night

at low tide I sat naked in the water
flesh and bones sifting into sand
I watched them disappear my foot my hand
there was nothing left of nothing my voice
I was anything a man a boy a woman in her dreams
thinking as usual of words to bring this surrender ashore

but there were no words
just this water burial
and eyes windows for light
until there was no seeing

until all the voices I'd been
slipped through the sky's blue hole in my head
and there was no saving me

nothing in the mirror

1.

something about all the rooms I have inhabited
the way they were cluttered cloisters
or how I sit cross-legged in this room today
eating oysters with my cat
reminds me of someone   or maybe a mirror

a woman lying on a narrow bed
moonlight slipping across the sill
touches the darkness of her eyes

she is asleep   unless
I look again
and begin to understand the wound
within her sleep

her endurance on that wind-swept terrain
where she stands alone in snow
remembering children at fox and goose

while others wonder at the memory
she wonders at its ruin
and then   because she has earned the strength she
    was given
she turns toward the light

she sleeps where she threw herself
skirt caught high on her thigh
dark hair across her throat

when she wakes she smiles
and rises   opening her blouse

2.

I heard a voice in the backyard
singing *das grab ist leer*

I went to the window
saw sheets and pillow cases flapping

the wind   in march
was cornflower blue

3.

something about the river
I heard ice grind in my sleep
something fierce and necessary
tempted me

sun rising in april
I stood on the assiniboine
heard ice boom in the distance
and suddenly cracks scattering around my feet
I waited for water to open beneath me

vater sterbt

a man with one blind eye
who meant well

tod

kalt

there was something about rivers
perhaps that each one held a reflection
waiting for me

wasser

she walked there
sometimes I met her

once I found her yellow scarf

4.

I was waiting at new year's
for the woman who knew every dance

waiting for midnight
when lights went out
and everyone kissed

a woman gave me her tongue
who was she?

I hid in another room
a window stood open
when I spoke I saw the clouds of words
how they vanished when I held my breath
I wondered at my foolishness
talking to myself
and snow drifting through the window

I saw her face against the glass
where she found me
my shadow and my silence

waiting for her
for whom everything happened a first time

I remember how her hands undressed me
while I stood shivering beside the bed

I thought it had happened before

5.

she knows I am a left-eyed son
seeking an end to memory

she knows I am an animal of temptations
that I want to disappear
at the hem of her flesh

she will not read my cards
laughs and invites me to read her eyes
they are grey

I see my hesitation there
as each step crumbles beneath me
this is how life falls apart
on the porch as I reach to knock
and time and again step aside
just when light falls from the opening door

I recognize my pale defiance
I tell her it's all I have

this is what she says
that I can dream of anything
babylonian women
a black dog
anapurna

that   somewhere between yes and no
I can answer for myself

that I will end
how my kind ends
looking for other conversations
in other rooms

6.

stepping from shadow
I shivered beneath a streetlamp
there was never enough light

someone was singing
from a cellar across the street

...im dunkeln wird mir wohler sein...

I was waiting for lili
she would be wearing a yellow dress

or caroline otero
her lemon breasts
and spanish obscenities

words teased me into her arms
they were fine linen
sometimes silk or valenciennes
I felt them with my fingers
but they slid away
before I could know I knew them
she took me into her lascivious bed

when I left I turned to the window
her oval face and dark hair
her red chemise
she was waving me goodbye

I raised my hand
but the sun shifted
and she was gone

7.

it's old-fashioned
being brave

ritter

always riding to another tournament

the usual true blue betrayals
meanness and small talk
but always   in the end   a need for honour

what else can a man do?
to find the woman
some days I catch a glimpse of her in my mirror

I follow

a stony river bed
an overgrown road

always riding past the tournament
into the desolate countryside

narr

8.

a pair of high heels
beside the stardust door

long beckoning fingers
saturn's wedding ring
and the overt stage

she lost her veils
asters blooming in the saxophone

I can't say it wasn't her
there was something familiar in the legs
they could leap mountains
but I had never before seen
the hunger in her eyes
and the fantasy in mine

9.

as if she knew I was standing outside the door
imagining her thighs or her slender back
she called me in   laughing
it wasn't the first time
she knew I loved to watch her undress

she was soaping her breasts
lifting
caressing
shaping them

she smelled of soap and spice
her hair was tied back

*I'm bathing for you
now you must bathe for me*

I removed my clothes
and stepped into the water
she reached up and drew me down

telling me about her day
she wrote in the water with her finger
as if I could read

I hadn't seen bare breasts all day
everyone out there wore clothes
I wanted to touch her beauty everywhere
and when she made a circle
with her index finger and thumb
I thrust my stick-up finger through

we had to laugh
the way our bodies came alive
and nothing much happening
how we knew our ways toward each other

we had to laugh
the way I wanted to relive life
like men before me   and sons
butting my way into the solar system

we had to laugh

10.

sometimes it begins with barking
a dog outside my window   or
the harsh bickering of jays

someone walking through my room
sets the globe quivering on its axis

niko knocks over a jar in the kitchen
I hear glass grind underfoot as he gets the broom

this is how I wake from my dream

this is when I begin to remember
the words I need

11.

she opens her lilac umbrella
and makes room for me

I can't help myself
it's the rain

somewhere it is midnight
and nothing in the mirror
a pillow slides to the floor

she hunches over him
one of them cries out   you can't tell who
they're lost in their helplessness

in the blind street outside
you can hear them mew and grunt
it's how you know where you are

but it drives you wild
wishing for love in a foreign city
long-legged women walking by
you imagine they're all passionate
in their rooms their clothes on the floor
kicking off their shoes
you imagine a room with six windows and maybe athenian light
you lie there in her bed
as she rides you past pleasure
until you can't take anymore
but you stay you want to stay
hinged like this

unhinged   somewhere
you are on the street
naked beneath her umbrella

it's the rain
it's everywhere
and I can't help myself

12.

her grey eyes gaze sometimes from my wall
or from the music in my room

she sends me postcards from the himalayas
a moon bear   a red panda

I keep meaning to ask if she's seen yeti
but the question never comes up
I think she's been there
though she pretends she hasn't
and she didn't take the photographs

often she is hard
and I think she hates me
but she's just angry
or doesn't care

she lets me off the hook
so to speak
she disengages me
to my captivity

there must be a better way to say
I don't want to lay down the cards

I remember now she was there
standing in front of a red stone house
she was wearing a silk top hat

one day I'll be there
on a treeless mountainside
giving up giving up

giving up

13.

there is something ahead
what I'm walking toward

around a corner
in a doorway

wherever my birthday waits

a pair of shoes

if she is there
they will fit

if it is the death of me

14.

oil spreads on the newspaper
my cat licks delicately at a last oyster

this week is nativity
next week the century continues on its grievous way

I am remembering the river

I am remembering
how the blouse slipped
from her shoulders

there is no other comfort

a dream of winter in her eyes
she puts her finger to my lips

a top hat at her feet

black river

dream of the black river

I'm dreaming a dream of the black river where I can't swim I'm
    dreaming my last breath I'm dreaming how things are almost
    over I'm dreaming a possible swimmer with powerful arms to
    hold me
the river is cruel and cold I would drown for warmth
my legs dangle beneath me in the water my hands perform circles
    my lips are open for a kiss who will kiss them?

a figure on shore I can make it out someone knows I'm out
    here someone appears poised on a rock a diver about to
    thread evening air and enter this dark water
but no one moves there is only a pose of intention and nothing
    happens ever again

my darling lord take me all the way my fishtailing body my
    hearing my faithful tongue
show me early morning first light across yellow fields could
    crack my heart
I had eyes enough to see it all blue eyes that didn't care except
    to see and see and see
I stood in the long grass and turned around and around it was
    all there all the love its earth and flight and the rain at night
move me again my darling I used to unlace my shoes and go
    barefoot I walked through grass felt the earthworm's trembling
    tunnel sometimes I was so light I walked above ground it
    made me laugh my legs streaming with power or light I could
    see it shining in my veins I was a snake sloughing his life
    with no hope for another there was nothing to want or need
    or do there was nothing

nothing feels like something when you straddle a bough high in
    the sugar tree or ma's singing in the kitchen
when you love someone feels so light you could walk without
    shoes anywhere you could doff your hat and fly

my love take me away all the way to where my lies are true
take me beneath your umbrella of water that will be good enough
    for me to stand in the rain dreaming the dreams of the dead
    and living dogs barking in backyards remembering the love
    and terror that brought me here
my beauty lay me down and take me all the way I'm dreaming
    the dream of my death or someone is it doesn't feel like me
    anymore
he's gasping the river is in his ears he's banging at the window
    he wants to break into the swimmer's dream he wants another
    another

evisceration

lord I'm coming apart this is the time of my evisceration this is
    when my singing ceases and something almost silent begins
I'm not safe in the night turning in my sleep I'm not safe throughout
    the day
in all weather in my walking or my talk in my room or when my
    heart is open there is no safety
I have danced and slipped I have fallen I have been cruel and I
    have lain in the arms of betrayal
everything has happened and I've gone nowhere I'm spinning
    you're not here you're not there
I'm bereft of love and sense I'm stupid in my collapse no one
    hears me I'm not saying the words that could make anyone
    see or know my descent
I'm bereft of words but not the need to find them

you may hear or not you may walk away still I will speak my fears
    I will admit the shoes and hats I wear
I'll be your fool take my foolishness and hold it up for me to know
I would drown for love because that's love it is hard and unrelenting
there is no return there is only the wall I walk toward

yesterday I threw my hat in the air today I wear it again gravity
    is not always a friend
I'm falling it's not this I fear it's falling forever
it's not love's refusal to forgive I fear I fear its absence
I fear my love will not reveal its true face I fear what I am in the
    night and what I conceal all day
lord I fear each breath I fear this paradise I do not fear death it will
    catch my fall

what do I ask where are you to hear there is emptiness everywhere
when I come to the end of myself when I stand at the basin and
    look through the window of the mirror what will I see?
give me ropes and water I will place them in my shrine
I will learn the love that tears me open
give me celestial burial my body spread-eagled and dispersed
    throughout the world
I will be your fool in the talons of an iron bird I will be free in the
    horrible sky

flicker and hawk

there are clocks that stand still there are doors that don't open
the summer has almost died and I won't grieve my angel's
      talking to me
I look up I look down I know where I am it's time to love again

love and anger inhabit all our rooms we should have torn apart
      years ago
what is this tenacity that makes us cruel and brings us together?
all argument and logic all sense tells us it shouldn't be
but here we are eyes meeting and I think I see you it's been
      months your eyes are harder now but something in them
      makes me shiver tonight something from that first recognition
      when you knew and wanted me
there's nothing I can do wariness falls away I would risk anything
      for that look it's what brought me here in the first place a
      tenderness
the door to my heart opens it swings open so easily I wouldn't
      have thought it possible
you step in you're a girl in a blue pleated skirt and white ribbons
      in your black hair I know your face you step in fearlessly
      and look about at the red and blue walls at bare furniture
      you sit cross-legged in mid-heart light from the open door
      falling on you I hear you laughing you're happy you're throwing
      kisses everywhere
is this why I'm here to give you room all the windows and the floor?
your kisses are free and burning I'm spread all over the room
      the sky woman everything rises or crashes around me and I'm
      willing to ride it out

lord history falls in the cracks that's a way of saying I don't
  believe a thing I haven't lived and known that I don't want
  to put my shoes on and I don't want to fly away
my hands are open my heart this is how I was born how I am
  when my man and boy stand
lord this love is strong even when it's on the edge when we find
  others to make us whole we're not everything to each other
  we're everything else and that's the juice you can't get every day

my sweet heart didn't we know all this time we stand apart we
  turn toward each other in our eyes all the love we know
  reaching for the adversary we see?
we are two people man and woman we are two cultures and two
  birds in different flights we are two elements
we have learned the odds and embrace them
we come together fire and water flicker and hawk this is what
  we know of love

forget every death

there is a woman I know who reads cards and throws coins
there is a woman who gets carried away sometimes I'd like to
    carry her away it doesn't always work that way she comes
    to me to remind her of her feet
there is a woman I know with beautiful feet

there is a woman I watch her undress she has delicate shoulders
    I want to yield to the need in me to her I don't know if
    it's possible if she can open her arms and legs to the man
    if I can surrender to woman both of us whores for each other
    crying profanities from the bed the sun revolves round in love
    with limbs and tongues and lips

the body has its reasons there is a mirror that is not a window
    and we see each other when we stop looking for a way out
there is a woman I yearn for her words sometimes I can believe
    her it goes a long way when it comes to love I don't believe
    a word
when she is free of everyone she has long legs and I believe
    everything she is

it's not that hard to fly I've done it now and then it's not hard
    to walk feet feeling the road still it's tougher than flying
    and when you think you're walking at heaven and you've got
    wings and you figure paradise is near it'll take your life you
    won't find it and who wants it there's enough death until you
    quit looking and then maybe it hits you between the eyes
    and it's got another name altogether another god another
    road or none at all

you can't tell sure turns you around how nothing's right nothing
        works sure can send you flying through the window
you can't tell your hands don't know a thing and you can't remember
        your eyes
can't tell a thing can you? can't tell a thing when your tongue's
        got amnesia when you can't find the facts or the story or what
        you've done with it and there's not much to hold on to

this is what happens these days sometimes when I put down my
        book undress and come to bed she arches for me in her sleep
        her mouth just open her breath is fenugreek I lean to kiss
        her and she arches her arms surround me her skin warm and
        smooth and my eyes and ears are full my heart I'm crying
        with everything spilling I don't know if I can take it all the
        pleasure and I can't help it and I do

there is a woman who loves me that's one way of saying it I
        find it hard to believe this isn't something I know a lot about
there is a woman who walks into the river I meet her on a good
        day we make love in august in the river in the water flowing
        between our legs her hair free at last I forget every death
        that has happened and slip downstream

breaking for light

I just stepped out of the cold dream that's it I won't be in
    dreams anymore
no more walls or webs it's not me in your cards I'm swimming
    upstream heading out of the dream
I'm no one's goat anymore I'm no dreaming joseph I'm thrashing
    through water half the time I'm drowning the rest of the way
    I'm breaking for light

I am myself when I write I know I've got the glory it spreads
    like heat from the heart sometimes I'm standing on my chair
    downstairs singing harmony or slow-shuffling around the room
    with smooth rhythm
it happens the lord's there no question and I take the words
    I'm hungry for the words there's love there someplace between
    the words
and I say them and sing them you can see the red and blue in
    the room
and I know where I am it feels clean no clothes no dreams I
    feel you my heart's open come on come on whoever you are

I know somewhere outside the room it's warm it's a place to find
    seems to me love is warm when it's not cold
froze my feet long ago it's not every day you thaw and come out
    smiling not every day love's born and grows old but it happens
you never called me lover you strung me along but I'm catching
    on to you I'm not in your dream I'm a lover and you're
    smiling in spite of yourself it's what you said you wanted
    all along can you take it?

you pull away just when I'm drawing near it's an old trick lord
    and I'm fooled again
there's no going back it's been too hard I've earned my touch
    I'm not going where it's cold
lord I've found earth and feet I'm out of dreams you're here by
    a thread

could be love we'll finally come out clear it's time and we're
    worn out
things falling around us the tricks the knife all the rage the night
it feels like last chance to bless our wounds and let them blossom

I'm asking can you take me straight on? I'm a lion some days a
    rabbit I'm not anyone else
can you take my kisses and my juice? I want you all the way
    sometimes at close quarters and at length I want to be everyone
    I am with you
when I'm lewd or unruly can you laugh? when I'm tender what then?
when the streetlight's in the window and the children asleep
    can you know my absence?

could be we'll come out clear I've fallen out of dreams there are
    no arms to hold me this is where I swim
you want to know where I am this is my hand this is how we
    touch is there anything else we could want?
I'm breaking for light I don't know what's next but I keep
    finding out

an audience with the dalai lama

after words

we're looking through the window knocking and waving for
    someone to see us but someone never shows not someone who
    can see everything lift a stone and smash the glass
we sit in the kitchen the telephone is quiet light goes down
children put themselves to sleep no stories no embrace who knows
    what the dark is to them tonight or what they'll dream

our life together an archive we descend each finding each
    unforgettable reference each festering memory and footnote
our words leap toward laws and customs we want the other
    to concede a deference to outside sources
when authority is denied we stare cold or fire black bullets of
    rage knowing we can't stop that this night's vengeance will
    find a home here in the kitchen the garden or some other
    place we live

we betray all the people we've been deny who we'll be
I don't know this voice I speak though I've heard it before
the room is destroyed by words I've thrown plates at the wall
    you're threatening me with a stone this must be what our
    children dream

wallpaper torn dishes underfoot I want the walls down but I know
    I'll need them
my rage scattered around me I stand where I stand I don't know
    anything else
I see the stone in your hand and I know your fear's diminishing
mine begins there's a seasoned killer in your face a killer without
    compassion or regret
as if you don't know me mother did this once looked through me
    as if I wasn't there for her I wasn't
this was an early death and necessary a tough rehearsal

I want to pity myself this juggernaut woman before me I want
    to adore what I don't know
I want to go home to my room a boy on mother's lap before
    she disowned him this must be how religion begins
I used to curse beneath father's hand we both did what had to
    be done and if it didn't have to be done we did it anyway
who am I in my rage with you some new father or old a broken-
    down lover?
am I everyone I have learned to distrust those faces in my mirror?

you don't throw the stone though you make a motion and I jump
it's better to murder there are men who would rather die than
    cringe
I've learned to swallow tonight before exhaustion our eyes growing
    hard we say what saves us human words that finally forget
    truth or resolution and give us time

this is a hard way it's how we move into the open where lightning
    or the forgotten animal can strike
it's where we hold those few almost useless words in hand walking
    next to naked from silence to silence
if we stay with it long enough when we wear out the pain if we're
    lucky break the glass and step out the stars come out clear
    and we hold hands
that's about the best love there is after words walking beneath
    streetlamps and stars
thankful for this night with each step the bride and groom wonder
    how it all works

epperson's cello

epperson's cello breaks through the formalities tonight I must be
   drunk about to make a fool of myself slack-jawed and pale-
   eyed I look around the table and see everyone's besotted
   and the music is weaving around our heads until only hearts
   are free
I know this is a great escape I've yearned for anything can happen
   this is a warm anarchy where all the flags fall down
we're breaking bread and drinking wine it sounds like a set-up but
   it's true it's happening and true is inadequate dvorak epperson
   and the cello are trinity
I must be drunk why else would I talk so predictably so
   sentimentally as if I'd given up all intelligence
I live with words I try to make them feel and I'm moving through
   cliché toward silence there's honour in this it's no lie yet I
   don't know that

I have no words for epperson's cello only words to surround it
   this isn't what I want
let's just say there's ice on the road I'm heading home and small
   cars are swimming all over the place from curb to curb careening
   across the st james bridge through traffic lights and northern
   lights it's way past midnight and this could be saturn with its
   rings or prague or winnipeg for sure
I'm wide open like a wound to the windshield and the moon
I'm going home and there's winter all around I'm going home to
   everything I know but the lights have changed
my tongue banging into my teeth my lips I want to kiss the wall
   the doorknob balancing on the keyhole where I crouch watching
   my love undress her body opens my eyes I watch my heart
   in her hand the happy thunder of my death it's my doing I
   remember watching mother watch the stars it was her undoing
   and somewhere in november with frost in the windows I saw
   grandfather suck on his smouldering cigarette

epperson's cello now I'm remembering was a gift he gave easily
    so easily could make you laugh
epperson's cello was a plumb line from head to foot a dream of
    divinity perhaps or all the clichés gone to bed and the human
    heart alone

the blue wind
for carol

albert street windows are mirrors this afternoon
a woman stops to see herself but the sun dips behind a cloud
    and she sees me instead
she's startled but doesn't turn she studies the possibilities of
    my face
it feels as if we're both watching a film maybe with oscar werner
    and simone signoret in it
I remember her eyes they're the blue eternity is when you're a child
the blue I dreamed in 1959 as the dalai lama crossed the himalayas
the blue piano in my home church on good friday morning
    and mother's soprano singing me toward resurrection

I'm not sure what's going on here whether it's remembering or
    words but something's running away with me and I don't mind
the woman's gone she may be blocks away thinking how our eyes
    met thinking that maybe we were in one of those european
    films where people meet through restaurant windows and make
    melancholy love all afternoon
maybe she's trying to remember where we've met before

I'm lost in the world yearning for black-haired women shaggy-
    haired black-haired women one who can heal with her hands
    another a lover in a red coat one who knows the day I will
    die and the one I just saw
explain it to me the woman who walked by her recognition
    her complete need for me and her indifference
explain this my sudden lust my laughter as the thin red doors of
    my heart rasp open and the blue wind blows through at last

listen to this stammering this voice as it caterwauls through its
    wounds and desire the barbed wire behind the eyes
listen to the heart today it's happy
this woman I know by the grace of mirrors I've seen her
an appearance in my life and my life bending like light as it
    passes earth

leaving home

orange peel on the sill a slow rain all day
you lean in the window looking at your garden how everything's
   happened there the rise and fall of every season you've known
you're thinking about the book you've read asking how van gogh
   lived so long through his abandonment there must have been
   a way for him out of his ferocious worship
how could a man knowing us to the marrow be alone how could
   he be so clear in the sloppy heart of paris?
you wonder about the movement of men and women in the galleries
   with their dandy clothes and need
you wonder about the louvre and prado the explosives gathered
   there you wonder about the vatican and parthenon the whole
   wild west striptease
it can't be put together can it?

you step out and things begin to fall away the window the porch
   your garden
you breathe and listen to each breath beneath the eaves as if it
   will bring a memory
as if you're standing on the rude ground where water broke and
   adonis fell between ma's hairy legs
you're standing in his birth brutalized by beauty kepler's telescope
   at your eye
you become a voyeur applauding the sistine ceiling reaching for
   the perfection of a muscular paradise
God and prophets in the blue sky orion's belt ursa minor the
   sculptor's workshop

it's an ecstasy of distances from your eyes to constellations
between today and tomorrow from your left to your right hand
you imagine the beauty you see there are such possibilities in
    these distances
you almost jump from your skin you want to reach out to what
    you see
maybe you will find yourself there   is this eros?   longing for
    consummation in another place on another day

you almost forget mother the old fossil she dressed so badly no
    manners and her smell somewhere between mammoth and
    ground sloth
you don't want to even think of it never mind father squatting
    on a stone his mouth dripping raw meat
ha you think that's how it was it's what you tell everyone the
    savage at the beginning of your quest
you don't want to know what came before him the intelligence
    and imagination the tumult of stone they gathered for god it's
    this you can't forget won't forgive their unspeakable sacraments

you want to you almost forget but memory itches and you scratch
 out a dream
ma and pa fucking on a riverbank you know they have to maybe
 seeing themselves in the water wondering for a moment who
 it is
pa likes to talk with the guys everything they've done gets better
 this way the fear and exhilaration the wounds fire and prayer
who knows what ma's doing digging in the ground sometimes
 bleeding her and the other women and kids they like to talk
 about seasons and smell and why
walking through the trees they all make their way into the open
 where the sky has them
you know ma and pa are oblivious to strategies of flesh sometimes
 they gaze at each other you know they don't mean anything
 by it not at first yet ma's unused breasts grow so full and
 ripe it drives them to spooning beneath the moon
and always there's talk with each new word they make the whole
 hairy naked bunch of them move relentlessly toward scriptures
 and love and death

this is when the dream comes home when everything today falls
 away and there's only singing like there's nothing in the words
 only the voice woven from wind and grass long ago
that's one for the books isn't it? how we take bone and heart
 lovingly and tell them toward goddess in song blessing I guess
 what we are
mummy and daddy without regret adonis where he dropped
 clutching his umbilical madame blavatsky at dawn or ninon de
 lenclos at the harpsichord

it won't be held against you how you dream your way back dreams
    too must vanish there is no judgement here and one day you'll
    find what it is you mean to find
perhaps the sound death leaves behind when you die and only
    hearing's left it could be any time in a twinkling let's say
    when you're bereft and weeping at the door or stark blind
    feeling your way among the trees toward ma and pa
you may find the river where you began before words when every-
    thing had to happen and ma and pa hesitated between love and
    necessity
and if you're blessed and someone embraces you with an
    unquestioning heart there's nothing more to find

your window's an open secret
his limbs wrapped around a bough your son sleeps in the willow
    dreaming of tyrannosaurus rex
your garden blossoms in the rain beneath your umbrella you're
    leaving home again

an audience with the dalai lama
or, the old-fashioned pas de deux

on the one hand a leaf in the shrub beside you
on the other family and work
I have never seen God I have been empty and filled and empty
    again

what can I say about what I know?
hymns that come easily to my lips while I walk
an ancient anger and the bags I carry filled with hats and shoes

I don't think I know much beyond what I know
my left my right hand a leaf wife and children
and sometimes a stony eye

my room you wouldn't believe the books and clothes all over the
    floor the records and stamps the lamp my smell around the typer
nothing much has happened there if you think of it and I have
on the other hand nothing more has happened outside the room
I grew up with lilacs there are lilacs outside my window there's
    not much I can make of that
it's like looking at old photographs in a way like catching a second
    wind or an animal in me sniffing out its old grounds

sometimes I think I have a question I want to have a question about
    things that matter
my body used to give me pleasure still does but it's beginning to
    break down maybe there's a question here
my knees my eyes sometimes there's a ringing in my ears and who
    knows what's happening just now in my most hidden cell a
    small detonation
but it seems clear where everything's going
I feel a lot more stupid than I did is this wisdom?

listen my love is someone other than me this must be what I need
she goes on journeys you should see her walk toward the clearing
    trees making way you should see her in her wedding dress the
    hem wet in the grass
you should see her when she drops the armour of her veils

when she's away and it's late when I crawl into bed I find she's
    dressed the emptiness beside me with her gown
all night I'm restless I wake when my hand finds silk my legs
    want to wrap around her
no bed has ever been this empty or so full it feels like god

a man can't say what he is that he needs to rut like a plow knows
    earth that he loves it
that he bends his knee to words he loves this too falls insensible
    sometimes before the beauty of memory and ruin
sir richard manuel died a lousy death hanging there cold as a fish
I can't explain it just listen to any of his songs just listen to how
    pure and sad a man's voice can be when he wants paradise
    but his arms aren't long enough
some voices belong to everyone

the boy in me doesn't like conversations he's busy wants to be free
    a word for what he remembers he could have said captured
    surrounded or surprised
he dreams time before love when he could sing the words didn't
    matter only the voice he was
but the man in me accommodates love and loss contemplates
    smoke and mirrors from a distance
he moves toward religion like prey to the lion a leaf to earth
    or a fish to the hook

does the prey feel ecstasy as it kneels into the lion's need? its
  stem hardening does the leaf desire release?
no I don't look for answers the questions are old and will grow
  older I want something other than rhetoric or ritual maybe
  a gesture
my devotion to the lord is imperfect there's some fight left in
  me I may be hooked I am not landed

what's there is my room my hands on the typer my eyes we used
  to say what's the diff
my children chewing at my knees my wife smiling through the
  window where's she going or is she coming home? she loves me
  she loves me not she loves me
what's there is the usual concoction hubble bubble eye of newt
  babbling tongue the old-fashioned pas de deux me and you

sometimes mother's on the phone do I love her yes I do and I
  still have father's hat
no I haven't seen God I live with angels some fallen
I sing *have thine own way lord* half the time I don't mean it
my wife sloughs her gown my pants at my knees like some clown
my son with his other world eyes you could never know them
  or their danger
or my daughter's prayers at night when everyone's asleep this is
  a way she speaks
and this is what I know what I need to know I want to redeem
  love before it does me in

private ceremonies

I have asked friends to perform private ceremonies in europe
one tossed a good luck stone into the aegean
another prayed for me in a white church near athens
later she sent a postcard from a pub in gdansk
someone walked to the harbour in barcelona and made a wish
this is how I travel europe with spells and invocation
I visit europe hidden in my friends' hair
or leaping from their passports at borders

I haven't been to europe my tracks cover another world it's taking
    me forever to cross a blue town beneath an electrical storm
    the highway's shoulders where I stuck my thumb out for freedom
    and this tenacious city
there are streets that have been paths where I grew up the
    street of sugar trees and caragana bushes the street that ran
    past the funeral home you could see a corpse lying in its
    coffin beneath dim light late at night and the street
    leading out of town
in this city streets where bookshops stand a small bar streets with
    chinese restaurants or an italian club streets without reproach
    streets where I carried my daughter on my back streets where I
    dreamed other lives

today my footprints are in this home where I've walked every floor
    the walls and ceilings where I've lain in bed sick in body or
    mind where I've tended fevers and imbalances where I've walked
    to the door for the mail or to test my memory with God's
    obnoxious people where I've talked and listened many ways with
    my love where I've carried my children to bed at night singing
    or telling where I've stalked around the typer or slithered like
    a snake where I've blundered late into bed or bellowed or wept
    in rage or pain or sorrow or tiptoed in and out of closets
    and conversations where I've crawled or swept toward sex
    where I've danced away fears or just for joy
I've brought my body and words here and my strength I've earned
    money this is where my music plays this is where I've broken
    and mended where I've learned several sides to love

friends there are wars here and there is unbearable delight each
    betrayal meets a loyalty who knows where it ends
I can't contain it all sometimes I'm beside myself often death's
    right there
my love and I talk late there are many other things we could
    be doing there are other lives for us to live but we've chosen
    each other there is an allegiance we take the time to talk
    and touch and we take the time to forgive
I'm here where I live and wrestle where I'm father for my children
    and everything I can be for love

one time around

it's raining at the window I can't tell which side there's thunder
    on the roof and sheet lightning in the sky
there's always something happening there's no one knows it all
someplace there's paradise they say but it's far away
nothing divine cares nothing gets me out of here yet the heart
    heals

I held a woman near I was thankful and filled with words she
    smelled my chaos still she cupped my ear with her hands
    and whispered love
I thought it really is that simple isn't it? though we've earned
    it for years
there's nothing perfect in what we know that's sure I hold no
    hope beyond our embrace in the doorway
tonight I hear her again as if she never left my ear and sometimes
    I whisper in hers sometimes I miss her even when she's near

the world is sad a bird can break your heart in the morning
    sometimes I'm too stupefied to pray
sometimes I'm heading for the trees some kind of shelter but I
    never get there it's not meant to be
these days I know hardly anything by its name I forget my dreams
    before I wake
there's nothing I know just that I won't betray my hands and tongue
    I won't betray desire that's all
I've heard rivers I've heard guitars I won't forget my daughter
    in the sweet posture of her sleep or my son in the morning
    with his flashing skates it's something to see

tonight I'm ready where is everyone? my fever's gone down I
   want to dance all night maybe I'll get lucky
hey ma it's not the end times I've got hot feet and next to
   nothing to say
my face is breaking into a smile there's no joke no story nothing
   like that just the walls smiling and someone knocking at the
   door and dreams beneath the floor let them flow they say
   themselves completely I don't need any more
hey ma it's one time around there's rain at the window and
   someone's lucky tonight

translations

warrior

stille nacht	silent night

nothing in the mirror

das grab ist leer	the grave is empty
vater sterbt	father dies
tod	dead
kalt	cold
wasser	water
...im dunkeln wird mir wohler sein...	I shall feel better in the dark
ritter	knight
narr	fool